SOMERSET
RAILWAYS

The History Press

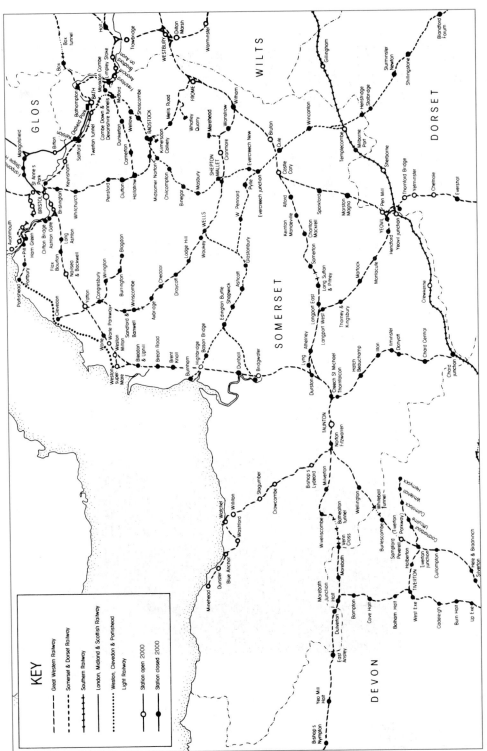

Somerset Railways

SOMERSET
RAILWAYS

TED GOSLING & MIKE CLEMENT

Dedicated to All the Railwaymen of Somerset

Templecombe station, 111 miles from Waterloo, is seen here in the Southern Railway days, looking east towards Gillingham. *(Lens of Sutton)*

First published in 2000
This edition published 2009

The History Press
The Mill, Brimscombe Port
Stroud, Gloucestershire, GL5 2QG
www.thehistorypress.co.uk

British Library Cataloguing in Publication Data.
A catalogue record for this book is available from the British Library.

ISBN: 978 0 7524 5212 8

Typesetting and origination by The History Press
Printed in Great Britain

Title page photograph:
Chard Junction seen from
the branch line. On the left
stands the main station
building, with the goods
shed further down. The
two-coach branch train is
just departing for Chard
Central and a newspaper
van stands in the siding.
(M.G. Clement Collection)

CONTENTS

Yeovil Town station, 19 August 1962. Drummond 0–4–4 'M7' tank No. 30131 from Yeovil Town shed (72C) is seen working the two-coach Yeovil Branch train (duty No. 517). The duty number is seen on the disc at the right of the smoke-box door. In the shed sidings are '57xx' class 0–6–0 pannier tanks No. 3733 and No. 4656. *(H.B. Priestly Collection)*

CHEDDAR (Somerset)

Map Sq. 22. Pop. 2,154. Clos. day Wed.

From Paddington via Westbury and Witham 128½ miles.

1st cl.—Single 43/8, Mth. Ret. 52/6.
3rd cl.—Single 26/3, Mth. Ret. 35/-.

Padd.	Ched.	Ched.	Padd.
a.m.		a.m.	
1 0	9 31	8 26	1 10
5 30	11 26	11 35r	4 5
9 15r	2 21	p.m.	
p.m.		3 15r	7 20
12 30r	4 40	6 34	4 15
3 30¶	8 32	—	—
—	—	—	—
—	—	—	—
—	—	—	—
—	—	—	—

Sunday Trains.

p.m.		p.m.	
1 20r	7 38	2 54r	7 55
—	—	—	—
—	—	—	—
—	—	—	—

¶ By Slip Carriage to Westbury.
ə Not Sat.   s Sat. only.
r Refresh. Car.

An excerpt from the 1949 Cheddar–Paddington timetable, taken from the April 1949 edition of *The A.B.C. Alphabetical Guide to Railways*, published by Thomas Skinner & Co., London. It was published monthly in book form, price 3s.

INTRODUCTION

The first railway to reach Somerset was the Bristol and Exeter. Bristol had already linked with London in 1841 and the line reached Taunton on 1 July 1842; it then carried on a further 8½ miles to Beam Bridge, where the boring of the Whitehall tunnel took place. The final stage of the 22 miles to Exeter was completed in the spring of 1844.

Somerset owes much of its development to the railway and, with the network reaching far and wide into the west, it was now possible to travel into what were once remote areas. The engineering of these early railways was truly remarkable, especially when you bear in mind that they were almost entirely built with pickaxes and shovels by gangs of navvies. The scale of their task was enormous and today it is easy to overlook this feat of engineering.

Before the Second World War, three major companies dominated the Somerset network: the Great Western Railway; the Somerset and Dorset joint railway and the London & South Western Railway. The Great Western operated throughout the county; the main line from Paddington, passing through Bridgwater, Taunton and

The naming ceremony of 'Merchant Navy' class 4–6–2 No. 35027 *Port Line* took place on 24 April 1950. No. 35027 came into service in December 1940 and was rebuilt in May 1957. It was finally withdrawn from traffic in September 1966. *(RAS Marketing)*

In a picture which relives the heyday of the steam age is 'King Arthur' class 4–6–0 No. 488 *Sir Tristram* in charge of an Up express approaching Crewkerne station, 2 August 1928. *(H.C. Casserley)*

Wellington to Exeter, with branch lines pushing out to Minehead via Norton Fitzwarren, Bishops Lydeard, Crowcombe, Stocumber, Williton, Watchet, Washford, Blue Anchor and Dunster; Chard Central to Taunton via Thornfalcon, Hatch, Ilminster and Donyatt; Yeovil Pen Mill to Castle Cary; Yeovil Pen Mill to Taunton via Martock, Langport, Athelney and Durston; and with stations in the north-west of Somerset at Avonmouth, Portishead, Clevedon and Weston-super-Mare.

Two companies merged to form the Somerset and Dorset Joint Railway, which crossed the county linking the north and midlands with the south and west of the country. The Somerset and Dorset joint railway main line ran from Bath Green Park to Templecombe via Evercreech Junction and then on through Dorset to Bournemouth West station. The individuality of the line made it popular with railway enthusiasts and it was affectionately known as the 'Slow and Dirty'. The line ran through country with as much enchantment as anyone could wish for, to lovely villages with names like Binegar, Midford, Wellow, Midsomer Norton, Chilcompton, Wyke Champflower, Pitcombe and Shepton Montague. Sadly, in March 1966 the Somerset and Dorset network was closed. The closure was much lamented and even today, over thirty years later, people still feel anger at the loss of this rail link.

The Southern Railway ran through Somerset on the Waterloo to Exeter main line, passing through such stations as Templecombe, Milbourne Port, Yeovil Town, Sutton Bingham, Crewkerne and Chard Junction, with branch lines from Chard Junction to Chard Central and from Yeovil Town to Yeovil Junction – and of course the link with the Somerset and Dorset at Templecombe.

Railway talk has a flavour of its own when it comes from the lips of men who served on the lines, and Mike Clement well remembers the time he served. In those days, no matter what company or region you worked for, you belonged to a big family. The railways never stopped, 24 hours a day, 7 days a week and 52 weeks a year. Becoming a railwayman meant that your life, and your family's life, revolved around the job: early turns, mid turns, late turns, Saturdays, Sundays, Bank Holidays – men were proud of working for the railway and served passengers with the courtesy and pride of those who know their jobs.

Working as a young fireman, Mike remembers the tales from the Somerset and Dorset enginemen. These tales are the oral traditions of other times, when men would bring bacon and eggs to work to fry up on a shovel on the footplate. If they were lucky to be working on shunting duties, there would be a chance to pick a few mushrooms to add to the feast. There was a certain magical quality about those days, when young cleaner-lads clubbed together to buy a packet of Park Drives or Woodbines to enjoy a cigarette with their cups of tea and sandwiches in the cleaners' cabin. With promotion to fireman came the comradeship of the engine-men's cabin, railway conversation, card games or shove-ha'penny and brewing up a can of tea ready for the road. With the heat and sweat on the footplate it was always recommended never to drink cold water, as this could give you painful stomach cramps.

An excerpt from the 1949 timetable for Minehead from Paddington via Taunton.

Perhaps it is foolish to try to recapture the spirit of such times, yet for railwaymen like Mike it was never quite the same after the Beeching axe and, with the end of steam locomotion, names such as GWR – 'Go When Ready' or 'Grub, Water and Relief; S&D – 'Slow and Dirty' and the SR – 'Shoddy Railway' – were all part of an era that disappeared.

On the last night of service on the Somerset and Dorset, just a few hours after the passing of the last service train, the Evergreen Junction North signal-box mysteriously burnt down. At the closing of the Yeovil Town engine shed the locomen came out in silence and burned their rule books in a brazier. Throughout the Somerset and Dorset line, and other branch lines, men paid homage, saying farewell to an age that had come to an end. Railwaymen with a lifetime of service had tears in their eyes, realising that they were leaving a job that was less a trade than a way of life.

The Somerset and Dorset Railway, with Somerset's branch lines, have long disappeared and today there is no sense of these lines ever being part of a rail network. It is now over thirty years since all this happened, and many of the men who worked on the lines have passed on. Mike himself left the railway in 1965 – he never did make it to the main-line gang, but he was a railwayman, and once a railwayman always a railwayman.

Templecombe lower platform, on the Somerset and Dorset joint railway, was built in 1887. The platform was immediately north of the London and South Western railway bridge which carried the Waterloo–Exeter line over the Somerset and Dorset Bournemouth–Bath line.

CHAPTER ONE

LOCOMOTIVES

A fine example from the Southern Railway days of steam traction. 'West Country' class No. 21C145 Ottery St Mary *on an Up train near Templecombe in 1947. No. 21C145* Ottery St Mary *was renumbered 30045 in January 1949, rebuilt in October 1958 and withdrawn from service in June 1964 after completing 761,465 miles. (R.M. Casserley Collection)*

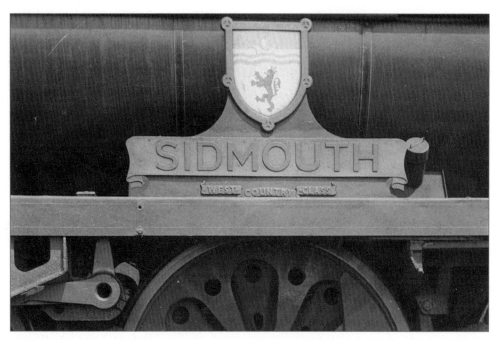

The name-plate and coat of arms on 'West Country' class (rebuilt) No. 340l0 *Sidmouth*. *Sidmouth* was built in 1946, withdrawn from service in 1964 and then left to decay in a Welsh scrapyard until 1982, when she was purchased for an aborted restoration bid at the North York Moors Railway. Southern Locomotives acquired the engine in 1999. *(M.G. Clement Collection)*

'West Country' class 4–6–2 No. 21C104 *Yeovil* was designed by Oliver Vaughan Snell Bulleid for the Southern Railway. This fine photograph shows *Yeovil* as new. Coming into traffic during June 1945, she was named at a ceremony in November 1945. *(National Railway Museum)*

'West Country' class Pacific No. 34033 *Chard* photographed at Exmouth Junction shed during August 1963. Originally numbered No. 21C133 under the Southern Railway, the engine came into service during June 1946. No. 21C133 *Chard* did not have a naming ceremony, and was finally withdrawn in December 1965 without ever being rebuilt. *(M.G. Clement Collection)*

A fine study of 'West Country' class No. 34040 *Crewkerne*, after she was renumbered by British Railways in October 1948. *(National Railway Museum)*

A fine picture of rebuilt 'West Country' class No. 34040 *Crewkerne*, taken at Bournemouth shed during the early 1960s. No. 34040 *Crewkerne* was rebuilt in October 1960 and finally withdrawn from service during July 1997. *(M.G. Clement Collection)*

Name-plate of 'West Country' class *Bere Alston*, which was renumbered 34104 in the BR numbering scheme in January 1950. *(RAS Marketing)*

'West Country' class No. 21C118 *Axminster* is seen here near Milborne Port during the summer of 1947. No. 21C118 was named *Axminster* at a ceremony which took place at Axminster station on 25 June 1946. *(Seaton Museum Photographic Archive)*

No. 34022 *Exmoor* was one of the 'West Country' class locomotives, some of which were given names of a Somerset area. *Exmoor* came in service on the Southern Railway in June 1946. The locomotive was rebuilt under British Railways during December 1957, and was withdrawn from traffic in April 1965. *(M.G. Clement Collection)*

Rebuilt 'West Country' class No. 34098 *Templecombe* came into service in December 1949. She was rebuilt in February 1961 and withdrawn from traffic in June 1967.

'West Country' class No. 21C141 on an Up express near Templecombe during the summer of 1948. No. 21C141 came into service in October 1946 and was named *Wilton*. In January 1949 she was renumbered 34041, and she was withdrawn from traffic in January 1966. During her time of rail service, 21C141 *Wilton* clocked up 626,417 miles. *(Seaton Museum Photographic Archive)*

'West Country' class No. 21C142, seen here near Templecombe in 1947, was named *Dorchester* at a ceremony which took place on 29 September 1948. The engine was renumbered 34042 in June 1948, rebuilt in January 1959 and withdrawn from service in October 1965. During her nineteen-year service, 34042 completed 726,761 miles. *(Seaton Museum Photographic Archive)*

Yeovil Town locomotive shed, August 1962. Standing in the shed roads are Bulleid 'Battle of Britain' class No. 34075 *264 Squadron* and 57XX class 0–6–0 pannier tank No. 3733, built by C.B. Collett. *(H.B. Priestley, M.G. Clement Collection)*

The Bulleid 4–6–2 'Battle of Britain' class locomotives served on the Southern Railway until the decline of steam in the 1960s. 'Battle of Britain' class No. 34070 *Manston* gleams on a spring morning in 1953. *(RAS Marketing)*

Name-plate of rebuilt 'Battle of Britain' class No. 34062 *17 Squadron*, with the Squadron crest and Latin inscription *Excellere Contende*. No. 34062 came into traffic in May 1947, was rebuilt in March 1959 and withdrawn from service in July 1964. *(RAS Marketing)*

When Winston Churchill made that memorable speech in the House of Commons during August 1940 and referred to the RAF, saying 'never in the history of human conflict has so much been owed by so many to so few', little did he think that a batch of forty-four locomotives would be named 'Battle of Britain' class. Shown here is No. 34066 *Spitfire* – what a splendid crest, and what memories are evoked by this name. No. 34066 *Spitfire* was withdrawn from service in September 1966. *(M.G. Clement Collection)*

'Battle of Britain' class No. 34070 *Manston* passes Sutton Bingham with an Up stopping train on a dull day in May 1962. Sutton Bingham reservoir can be seen on the left. *(C.L. Caddy)*

Yeovil Engine Shed yard, 19 August 1962. On shed are 'Battle of Britain' class No. 34075 *264 Squadron* from Exmouth Junction shed (72a), with 'S15' class No. 30827 and GWR pannier tank No. 3733 from Yeovil Town shed (72c). *(H.B. Priestley, M.G. Clement Collection)*

'Merchant Navy' class No. 35012 *United States Lines* name-plate. Each of the 'Merchant Navy' class name-plates carried the shipping-line flag in the centre. When Mike Clement was at Exmouth Junction shed early in 1965, the 'Merchant Navy' name-plates came up for sale when the locomotives were withdrawn from service. Today these name-plates from scrapped locomotives are the railway collectors' 'Holy Grail' – Mike could have bought them then for about £50 a piece. *(RAS Marketing)*

The great days of the Atlantic Coast Express were during the inter-war years of the Southern Railway, but it continued in service into the early 1960s. For a countless number of holiday-makers this was the way to travel to the West Country holiday resorts. In this splendid photograph, taken in 1960, 'Merchant Navy' class No. 35026 *Lamport and Holt Line* is approaching Milborne Port Halt down the 1 in 170 bank from Templecombe. Mike Clement, once a cleaner on the railways, noticed the grime on top of the boiler of 35026. This was because the cleaner lads could not reach over the top of the boiler when cleaning the engine – a job for tall lads only. (*G.A. Richardson*)

Streamlined 'Merchant Navy' Pacific No. 21C7 *Aberdeen Commonwealth* is pictured in full cry on an Up express near Templecombe during the summer of 1948. The driver, looking out from his cab, is wearing the engine man's SR brass cap badge. *(Seaton Museum Photographic Archive)*

'Merchant Navy' class No. 21C3 *Royal Mail* heads an Up express near Templecombe in 1946. *(Seaton Museum Photographic Archive)*

Mighty 'Merchant Navy' Pacific No. 35004 *Cunard White Star* dwarfs an 0–6–0 pannier tank in the sidings at Yeovil Town during June 1962. *(G.W. Sharpe)*

The name-plate pictured here is one of the batch of thirty 'Merchant Navy' class locomotives named after British and Allied shipping lines of the Second World War. This nameplate was on No. 35022 *Holland America Line*, rebuilt in June 1956. Mike Clement remembers well that when he was a cleaner at Exmouth Junction shed these engines took pride of place and were always well cleaned, with special attention paid to the name-plates. *(RAS Marketing)*

The 'Merchant Navy' locomotives were the pride of the Southern and worked all the express trains from London to the West. These engines were excellent performers and the top link men that handled them acquired a special mystique. This picture shows the name-plate of the last of the class built, No. 35030 *Elder-Dempster Lines*. This locomotive was rebuilt by British Railways Southern Region in April 1958, and was withdrawn from service in July 1967. *(M.G. Clement Collection)*

One of the regular 'Merchant Navy' class locomotives which worked the West of England main line was *Elders Fyffes* No. 35016, seen here in about 1958. There were thirty 'Merchant Navy' locomotives in the class, numbered from 35001 to 35030. *(G.W. Sharpe)*

An unidentified 'King Arthur' class locomotive approaches Templecombe with a Down fast for Exeter, *c.* 1939. It was piloted by T9 class No. 117. *(S.C. Townroe, M.G. Clement Collection)*

The romance of the Southern Railway during the days of steam is demonstrated in this picture. It shows a scene once commonplace but now almost totally unfamiliar. In this splendid photograph, taken on 22 August 1935 at Milborne Port, the photographer successfully caught Maunsell 'King Arthur' class No. 456 *Sir Galahad* thundering through the station, with safety valves blowing at 200 lb per square inch, with the twelve-coach first portion of the Down Atlantic Coast Express. *(National Railway Museum)*

A close-up picture of the name-plate of 'King Arthur' class No. 30448 *Sir Tristram*. Originally Southern Railway No. 448, *Sir Tristram* was built at the Eastleigh Works by Maunsell in May 1925 and worked over the Southern Railway and Regions for thirty-five years, until finally withdrawn from traffic in August 1960. *(Seaton Museum Photographic Archive)*

Another ghost of transport past – 'King Arthur' class 4–6–0 No. 741 *Joyous Gard*. One of the locomotives that graced the Southern West of England main line is pictured here in pristine condition in 1933. *Joyous Gard*, one of the Urie build batch of 'King Arthurs', came into traffic in May 1919 and was withdrawn from service during February 1956. *(M.G. Clement Collection)*

The distinctive quality of the great days of steam is captured in this photograph of 'King Arthur' class No. E777 *Sir Lamiel*, heading westward with the Down Atlantic Coast Express, April 1931. The Atlantic Coast Express was essential to holiday traffic and was Waterloo's answer to Paddington's Cornish Riviera Express. This picture was taken during its heyday. *Sir Lamiel* was saved from the scrapyard and today is the only 'King Arthur' class locomotive in preservation. *(RAS Marketing)*

In the summer of 1958 'King Arthur' class 4–6–0 No. 30449 *Sir Torre* was photographed on shunting duties at Yeovil Town: the signal-box is in the background. *Sir Torre* came into service with the Southern Railway in 1925 and was withdrawn from traffic under British Rail in December 1959. *(R.M. Casserley)*

One for all railway enthusiasts, to bring back memories of the great days of steam. No. 745 *Tintagel*, looking splendid, was captured by the camera in October 1933. She was one of the 'King Arthur' class locomotives that ran over the West of England main line for many years. *(RAS Marketing)*

Running light engine, tender first, we have 'N' class 2–6–0 No. 31845 passing Broom Gates on the Up line to shunt at Chard Junction, 18 July 1964. The Exeter–Salisbury head code is on the tender, the two discs top and bottom. *(M.G. Clement)*

The 'Schools' class engines were designed by Richard Maunsell for the Southern Railway in 1930. They weighed 109 tons 10 cwt and numbered 900 to 939 (30900 to 30939 under British Railway). They occasionally worked the main line west of Salisbury and were very reliable. Shown here is 'Schools' class 4–4–0 No. 30932 *Blundells*. *(M.G. Clement Collection)*

One of Richard Maunsell's 'Schools' class 4–4–0 No. 30912 *Downside*. The forty engines in this class were all named after public schools and saw service as Southern Railway express passenger engines. *(M.G. Clement Collection)*

A rare visitor to the Waterloo–Exeter main line was caught by the camera of Roger Joanes on 12 September 1961. 'Schools' class 4–4–0 No. 30912 *Downside* departs Templecombe with a train for Yeovil. *(Roger Joanes, Joanes Publications)*

A fine picture of one of the 'Lord Nelson' class 4–6–0 express passenger locomotives. They were built by R.E.L. Maunsell and introduced in 1926. Sixteen locomotives were in the class numbered from 850 to 865 during the Southern Railway period, and they were later renumbered under British Railway Southern Region as 30850 to 30865. Until the introduction of the Bulleid Pacifics they were the most powerful express locomotives on the Southern. They were all named after famous Sea Lords of the British Navy, and here we have *Lord Rodney*, No. 30863. *(M.G. Clement Collection)*

This name-plate was on 'Lord Nelson' class 4–6–0 No. 30858 *Lord Duncan*. No. 30858 came into service on the Southern Railway during January 1929 and was withdrawn under British Railways Southern Region in August 1961. *(M.G. Clement Collection)*

The locomotive standing in Templecombe lower yard during 1947 was one of the Southern Railway 'S15' class mixed traffic engines, No. 823. A total of forty-seven locomotives were in this class, designed by R.W. Urie and R.E.L. Maunsell. *(Seaton Museum Photographic Archive)*

Drummond 'L11' class No. E170, of Exmouth Junction shed, climbs to the top of Hewish summit *en route* to Salisbury, 2 August 1928. *(H.C. Casserley)*

'U' class 2–6–0 No. 1793 approaches Milborne Port during the spring of 1935, on a five-coach Up stopping train. Nos 1790 to 1809 were originally 2–6–4 tank engines from the South Eastern and Chatham Railway, and were named after rivers. No. 1793 was then A793 *River Ouse*. On 24 August 1927 'River' class No. 800 *River Cray* left the rails with the 5 p.m. Canon Street to Folkestone at Sevenoaks. Thirteen people were killed and twenty-one seriously injured. As a result of this accident the 'River' class tank engines were withdrawn and converted to tender engines. *(Seaton Museum Photographic Archive)*

Yeovil engine shed, 19 August 1962. In the foreground is 'N' class 2–6–0 No. 31802 from Yeovil shed; in the background is an unidentified Bulleid Pacific with a glimpse of a GWR pannier tank. *(H.B. Priestley/M.G. Clement Collection)*

The Somerset and Dorset's best-known train was the Pines Express, which was a vital link for holiday-makers from the Midlands to Bournemouth and South Coast resorts. The green-liveried Standard 5MT 4–6–0 No. 73054, from Bath Green shed (82F), regains the single line at Templecombe No. 2 box. It pulls past the Templecombe locomotive shed to go on under the Southern Waterloo main line with the Down Pines Express on 27 April 1961. On shed are 'WR' class 3MT 0–6–0 of the '22XX' class No. 3215 and Fowler 0–6–0 Jinty tank 3F No. 47542. *(G.A. Richardson)*

This outstanding picture was taken by Henry Casserley on 2 August 1928. It shows Urie 'H15' class No. E332, working an Up West of England–Waterloo express, passing the distant signal for Crewkerne Gates to enter the gloom of Crewkerne tunnel. The fireman on the footplate would be ready to shut the firehole door and knock the blower on, a necessary job because the roof of the Crewkerne tunnel was low, which drove the exhaust back down. This would have resulted in a blow-back from the fire on the footplate if the fire door was open. *(H.C. Casserley)*

Drummond 'L11' class 4–4–0 mixed traffic engine No. 145, of Yeovil Town shed, 28 August 1940. *(H.C. Casserley)*

CHAPTER TWO

THE MAIN LINES

With a halo of smoke and steam, Drummond 'L11' class 4–4–0 mixed traffic engine emerges
from the eastern end of Crewkerne tunnel at the head of an Up goods train, 2 August 1928.
Crewkerne tunnel, a distance of 132 miles and 39 chains from Waterloo, was 205 yards long.
(H.C. Casserley)

An interesting picture of Templecombe (Southern Railway) in the 1930s. In the station an Up passenger train waits, while a West of England goods hauled by 'S15' class No. 827 stands in the Down platform. *(H.B. Priestley, M.G. Clement Collection)*

Templecombe, 11 March 1961. Standard class 4 mixed traffic engine 2–6–0 No. 76068 of Eastleigh shed (71A) departs on the Somerset and Dorset line with the 3.58 p.m. to Bristol Templemeads. In the background Standard class 5 4–6–0 No. 73047 drifts in at the head of a Down train. *(M.G. Clement Collection)*

The 'Merchant Navys' were magnificent locomotives. Here on the bank 1 mile east of Templecombe, in 1947, 'Merchant Navy' Pacific No. 21C7 *Aberdeen Commonwealth* hauls the fourteen-coach Pullman *Devon Belle* on its journey from Waterloo to Ilfracombe and Plymouth. When the train arrived at Exeter Central it was divided, to be hauled by 'West Country' class Pacifics to respective destinations. *(Derek Winkworth)*

The *Devon Belle*, in full flight, steams away from Templecombe in 1947, hauled by 'Merchant Navy' class No. 21C4 *Cunard White Star*. *(Seaton Museum Photographic Archive)*

With Milborne Port station in the background, 'West Country' class heads an Up West of England–Waterloo express in 1947. No. 21C144 was only twelve months old when this picture was taken, and was later to be named *Woolacombe*. *(Seaton Museum Photographic Archive)*

A fine railway picture of excellent composition shows 'King Arthur' class 4–6–0 No. 789 *Sir Guy* hauling nine coaches with a West of England express heading down the bank approaching Templecombe in 1939. *(S.C. Townroe, M.G. Clement Collection)*

'Merchant Navy' class No. 21C10 *Blue Star* heads westward with the Down *Devon Belle* near Templecombe in the summer of 1947. The black smoke testifies that the fireman is hard at work on the footplate. The Southern Railway vigorously promoted the West Country as a holiday resort and the *Devon Belle* was introduced in June 1947 to run between Waterloo, Plymouth and Ilfracombe. During the early years the *Belle* was often loaded to fourteen coaches, totalling some 550 tons. The *Devon Belle* became a part of railway history when it was withdrawn from service after the end of the 1954 season, a casualty to increased road traffic. *(Seaton Museum Photographic Archive)*

Hurrying away from Templecombe station on a winter's day in 1946 we have Drummond 'T9' class 4–4–0 No. 727 with a stopping train to Yeovil. No. 727 came into service with the London and South Western Railway in 1898. In 1902 the locomotive was allocated to Dorchester shed and in May 1925 was painted in the Southern Railway livery. In February 1950, 727 was painted in BR lined black and renumbered BR No. 30727. The engine was allocated to the Salisbury shed and was withdrawn from service in 1958 after a working life of sixty years. *(Seaton Museum Photographic Archive)*

A Bulleid Pacific runs into the Up platform at Templecombe, *c. 1955. (H.C. Casserley)*

Another view of Templecombe station when it was still an important place, 11 March 1961. 'Merchant Navy' class No. 35009 *Shaw Savill* of Exmouth Junction shed (72A) runs into Templecombe at the head of the 7.30 a.m. Exeter Central–Waterloo, while Standard class 5 No. 73047 waits with a train on the line affectionately known as the Slow and Dirty (Somerset and Dorset). *(H.B. Priestley, M.G. Clement Collection)*

This scene of Milborne Port Halt, looking Up towards Templecombe, was taken in the 1950s. Milborne Port was 2 miles 45 chains west of Templecombe and 114 miles 31 chains from Waterloo. This view shows the Up platform, with footbridge over the line, and a shelter. On the Down side stands the signal-box, booking office and the stationmaster's house. *(M.G. Clement Collection)*

Sutton Bingham station, 16 July 1958. On a summer morning 'Battle of Britain' class No. 34081 *92 Squadron* runs into the Up platform on a stopping train. In a picture with a rich array of period detail, two ladies are ready to board the train for a shopping excursion to Yeovil. Four 5-gallon water churns stand on the Up platform, and there is a bag of tools at the bottom of the signal-box steps. *(H.C. Casserley)*

The special quality of railways of the past is caught in this photograph, taken at Wayford Bridge, not far from Crewkerne. The picture dates from around 1950 and shows a 'Merchant Navy' Pacific hauling the Down *Devon Belle*. The *Devon Belle* ran between Waterloo, Ilfracombe and Plymouth during the summer months. The display of wild flowers on the embankment is reminiscent of the pre-war hay fields. These banks were cut by permanent way staff with scythes. *(M.G. Clement Collection)*

A view from the ladder of the Down signal post at Crewkerne Gates, looking west towards Crewkerne tunnel, *c.* 1964. The gates can be seen in front of the coloured light signal on the Up side. *(M.G. Clement Collection)*

The old London and South Western signal-box is prominent on the platform in this photograph of Crewkerne station, 6 September 1959. 'Battle of Britain' class No. 34100 *Sir Trafford Leigh Mallory* can also be seen running in with the 3.20 p.m. Exeter Central–Yeovil Junction stopping train. The milk tanks on the back of this train were either from the Express Dairy at Seaton Junction or Wilts United Dairy at Chard Junction. *(H.B. Priestley, M.G. Clement Collection)*

The image of a train drawing into a station with steam billowing from its funnel is one that was relegated to nostalgia when the last steam trains were withdrawn in 1968. Photographs remain, however, and here is S15 class No. 30824 running into Crewkerne station at the head of a Down stopping train, 14 August 1958. A locomotive is busy in the Up yard of the sidings. *(H.B. Priestley, M.G. Clement Collection)*

Hewish Gates, seen here on 2 August 1928, was 1 mile 36 chains to the west of Crewkerne tunnel and 134 miles .04 chains from Waterloo. Passing Hewish box is No. 456 *Sir Galahad* with an Up West of England–Waterloo express. *(H.C. Casserley)*

Here is Mike Clement's favourite photograph. Drummond 'T9' 4–4–0 express passenger locomotive No. 284 heads a Down relief portion of the Atlantic Coast Express down Hewish Bank, *c.* 1925. *(H.C. Casserley)*

The 'King Arthurs' formed an important part of the Southern express passenger trains from the mid-1920s until 1960. These magnificent engines were much photographed and here in full glory we have 'King Arthur' class No. 789 *Sir Guy*, pictured just before the Second World War. The engine heads an Up West of England express, and is climbing up to Hewish summit. *(Seaton Museum Photographic Archive)*

A fine record of Hewish Gates, 2 August 1928. Hewish Gates was situated between Chard Junction and Crewkerne stations. In this photograph one of Dugald Drummond's 4–6–0 mixed traffic engines of the 'H–15' class, No. 330, is passing the Hewish signal-box on a Down express. Just to the right of the signal-box in the background can be seen the signalman's cottage, which belonged to the railway company. *(H.C. Casserley)*

The level-crossing gates were open to road traffic when this photograph of Chard Junction was taken, *c.* 1955. *(M.G. Clement Collection)*

Chard Junction station, 18 May 1959. Coming out from Chard Branch on to the Up main line is BR 2–6–2 class 3 mixed traffic tank engine No. 82011 hauling a seven-coach special day-excursion from Taunton to Seaton. Having cleared the Up catch point, the train would come back on the Down crossover line. *(R.J. Sellick)*

Western 2–6–2 tank No. 5503 of the '4500' class prepares to leave Chard Junction on a dismal winter's day, 23 February 1952, with its two-coach train for Chard Central. *(H.B. Priestley, M.G. Clement Collection)*

A photographer clearly accomplished in his composition of railway pictures successfully captured Bulleid 'Merchant Navy' Pacific No. 35012 *United States Line* approaching Chard Junction in July 1962, with an eleven-coach Waterloo–West of England express. You can almost hear the screaming whistle of the express and feel the way it roared through the station. *(Peter Barnfield)*

On a wet July day in 1962 Maunsell 4–6–0 'S15' class No. 30843 drifts into Chard Junction at the head of a Down stopping train for Exeter Central. *(Peter Barnfield)*

Maunsell 'S15' class No. 30823 runs into Chard Junction on a wet day during July 1962, with a local stopping train from Exeter Central. A large crane is visible in the goods yard. *(Peter Barnfield)*

WESTON-SUPER-MARE (Som)

Miles 136¾. Map Sq. 22.
Pop. 28,555. Clos. day Thur.
From Paddington via Bristol.
1st cl.—Single 46/6, Mth. Ret. 56/3.
3rd cl.—Single 27/11, Mth. Ret. 37/6.

Padd.	West.	West.	Padd
a.m.		a.m.	
5 30	9 46	7 0r	10 10
7 30r	10 55	8 20r	11 20
9 5r	12 15	8 46	12 40
9 15sr	1 15	11 12r	2 20
9 15er	1 24	p.m.	
11 15r	2 5	12 41sr	4 25
p.m.		2 18r	5 45
1 15r	4 20	3 30er	6 40
1 18	5 27	4 35r	8 15
2 15	6 25	5 42	9 35
2 35	6 52	6 50	10 50
5 5r	7 55	8 15	4 15
5 13	9 20	10 40	7 25
6 30r	9 45	—	—
6 35r	12 5	—	—
11 50e	7 10	—	—
11 50s	7 37	—	—

Part of the 1949 timetable for Weston-super-Mare from Paddington via Bristol, taken from the *A.B.C. Railway Guide*.

Yeovil Town station is on the left, and the top of the engine shed can just be seen on the far right, *c.* 1962. Four engines are in the loco sidings; at the rear is an 0–6–0 pannier tank, then a Maunsell 2–6–0 'N' class and then two Maunsell 4–6–0 mixed traffic and freight locomotives of the S15 class, one of which is No. 30826. *(H.B. Priestley, M.G. Clement Collection)*

Rebuilt 'West Country' class No. 34098 *Templecombe* at Yeovil Town station during 1962. In this view looking towards Pen Mill you can see the signal-box on the right, with part of the town beyond it. The fields on the left are going up to Ninesprings Hill. *(H.B. Priestley, M.G. Clement Collection)*

CHAPTER THREE

STAFF

A group of railwaymen break from their duties for this formal portrait. They were all staff members at Crewkerne station, and the patriarchal figure sitting in the middle of the front row was the station master. The year was 1906 and the London and South Western Railway poster in the background advertises the Bridport–Beaminster–Crewkerne horse-drawn bus.
(M.G. Clement Collection)

A fine record, giving an insight into the private working world of the railways. Hardington signal-box is pictured here in 1952, and signalman David Pettitt is looking out of the box window in a photograph taken by his wife. This box was reached by a mile-long track from Hardington village and was situated on the Up side 3 miles 30 chains west of Sutton Bingham. At one time the box controlled three sidings and a milk dock. The sidings came into use on 8 January 1909 and were closed on 7 February 1937. From that date until the box closed in 1959 Hardington remained open as a section box during the hours 9 a.m. to 5 p.m. *(M.G. Clement Collection)*

A picture that reflects the everyday life of people in locomotive depot offices before the Second World War. List clerk Reg Bartlett is undertaking his daily duties. Until recently the value of such photographs was not recognised and many were destroyed. Today, however, there has been a dramatic change, and people now appreciate the value of them. This photograph was taken at Yeovil Locomotive Depot. *(S.C. Townroe, M.G. Clement Collection)*

Signalman Fred Gibbs on duty in the new signal-box at Crewkerne station. The old London and South Western Railway box closed on 6 November 1960, the new one opening on the same day. This new signal-box had a life span of seven years, closing on 26 February 1967 after the Exeter to Salisbury line was reduced to a single track. *(M.G. Clement Collection)*

Traffic staff at Crewkerne station took great pride in their work and are relaxing in the summer sun on 16 August 1952. Left to right: George Riglar, Harry Peterson, station master Mr Cobley and Ben Smallden. *(M.G. Clement Collection)*

April 1965, and the permanent way department are in the process of tamping and aligning of the Up main-line track between Chard Junction and Crewkerne. *(M.G. Clement Collection)*

Inspector Hubert Pike, standing in the foreground and wearing the trilby hat, carefully watches permanent way staff turning the Plasser machine on its own hydraulic jacks at Chard Junction during April 1965. *(M.G. Clement Collection)*

Hubert Pike was one of those men, so few and far between today, who took a tremendous pride in his job. He was an inspector in the permanent way department, and is pictured here at work on the track bed at Chard Junction in 1965, measuring the gap and distance between the rails on the Down line. *(M.G. Clement Collection)*

Photographs like this showing a scene of everyday work, although of little interest at the time they were taken, are today visually valuable. Taken in April 1965, it shows in the foreground Inspector Hubert Pike with gangers Doble, Summers, Rolfe and Lombard in the background working between Broom Gates and Chard Junction on the Down line. *(M.G. Clement Collection)*

The staff at Templecombe face the photographer in an alert and confident manner for this group photograph, taken in 1921. The taking of large-group photographs is not easy: persuading everyone to look at you and keep their eyes open can be difficult. Here we have a picture so successful that you could almost reach out to touch the people. One of the men pictured here, sitting third from left in the front row, came to an unfortunate end when, during a Second World War air raid on Templecombe goods yard, he was blown to pieces. *(M.G. Clement Collection)*

A summer afternoon during August 1946, and signalman Bill Poole stands at the top of the steps of Hewish Gates signal-box. On the door frame behind are the letters LP9 37, which meant that the signal-box was last painted in September 1937. Railways were in the family, and Bill Poole had a son, Ron, who worked for the signal and telegraph department at Yeovil Junction. *(A.E. West, M.G. Clement Collection)*

'Drummond T9' class No. 30706 from Yeovil shed is here on shunting duty at Crewkerne station, 16 August 1952. The Yeovil men on the footplate are: left, driver John Gillham, and right, fireman Gordon Woolmington. At a later date in his railway career Gordon Woolmington was involved in a horrific accident, in which he acted with great courage. While firing the engine of an Up train to Yeovil Junction, he was working the pricker through the fire. Passing Hardington Bottom he withdrew the pricker with his hand, holding the iron ring at the top of this tool, and went to swing it up on to the tender. Unfortunately a Down train passed at speed and caught the long pricker, and the force of the two trains passing tore off his lower right arm and hand. He alerted the engine driver, Harry Churchill, who applied a tourniquet to the arm, and on arrival at Sutton Bingham told the station staff to ring through to Yeovil Junction to have an ambulance ready. On arrival at Yeovil Junction Gordon Woolmington walked unaided from the footplate to the waiting ambulance. He returned to work on the railway as a fireman on the Yeovil branch line, after having an artificial limb with a hook and claw fitted. *(A.E. West, M.G. Clement Collection)*

Another of those fine documentary photographs that show the closed-off, private working world of the railway. This picture was taken in 1939 inside the Yeovil shed by shedmaster Stephen Townroe, and a Drummond 'T9' with an 'N' class locomotive can be seen. The busy railwayman is a boiler washer, who is washing down the pit to clear away scale after a boiler wash-out of one of the engines. *(S.C. Townroe, M.G. Clement Collection)*

A picture of railway life that attracts immediate interest. At Yeovil Town locomotive depot, just before the Second World War in 1939, one of the Adams '0–2' class branch engines can be seen under the lifting hoist. A pair of driving wheels from the engine can be seen over the pit. The Adams '0–2' class 0–4–4 locomotives weighed in at 46 tons 18 cwt. *(S.C. Townroe, M.G. Clement Collection)*

Yeovil Town locomotive depot in 1939: an unidentified 'U' class 2–6–0 mixed traffic engine is being prepared for the road. These engines, designed by Richard Maunsell, weighed in at 110 tons 14 cwt and were introduced to the Southern Railway in June 1928. They were used on all types of duties and during the summer months, if the need arose, were used on express passenger trains. *(S.C. Townroe, M.G. Clement Collection)*

Smiles all round in this picture of permanent way and traffic staff at Crewkerne station below the signal-box, *c.* 1955. Left to right: Lengthman George Holt, traffic staff Harry Peterson, Gerald Russell and Rodney Haines. *(M.G. Clement Collection)*

Two permanent way gangers stop work to pose for this photograph some time during the early 1940s. They are seen here with the tools of their trade – a long spanner for tightening the rail bolts and a hammer for knocking in the keys. Left, Mr Banfield, and right, Mr Perrett. *(M.G. Clement Collection)*

Men of the permanent way department were vital to the running of a railway and, although the work was hard and unglamorous, they took a great pride in their job. In this picture, taken between Chard Junction and Crewkerne in 1965, men of the permanent way department are in the process of unloading a ballast train. *(M.G. Clement Collection)*

CHAPTER FOUR

HIGH DAYS & EVENTS

The naming ceremony of 'West Country' class Pacific No. 21C140 Crewkerne took place at Crewkerne station on 20 October 1948. After the ceremony some of the station staff posed in front of the engine for this photograph. Left to right: Mrs Nellie Salter holding her son Robert, who, when he grew up, became a fireman at Yeovil; Mr Tom Salter, a goods checker at Crewkerne; Jim Walbridge, signalman; and Charlie Osborne, station lorry driver.
(M.G. Clement Collection)

Such a sight will never be seen again. Southern Railway officials, members of the council and the people of Crewkerne gather on the platform at Crewkerne station. The Second World War had not long finished and many ambitious schemes were to feature in post-war development of the railways. This is the naming ceremony of 'West Country' class No. 34040 *Crewkerne*. *(National Railway Museum)*

Crewkerne station was the scene of a get-together on 13 January 1965, when the traffic staff gave a farewell presentation to Station Master Colin Cheesley. Left to right: Tom Salter, Bernard Powell, Jack Caldicott, unknown junior porter, Station Master Colin Cheesley, Eric Bowditch, Cyril Elliot, Gerald Russell, Robert Hill, unknown junior porter, Fred Gibbs and Frank Morris. *(M.G. Clement Collection)*

Templecombe station, looking east towards Gillingham, July 1906. *(Lens of Sutton)*

On 17 June 1964 British Rail withdrew its service from Yeovil Town to Taunton, via Langport, Athelney and Durston. Inspector Harry Watford is seen standing on the platform at Yeovil Town station, watching railway enthusiasts hang a wreath on the bunker of Western 2–6–2 tank of the 4500 class No. 4593. This train was the last one to run over this route. *(M.G. Clement Collection)*

This shows damage to the Up track at Crewkerne station, which occurred on 23 April 1953. Unrebuilt 'Merchant Navy' class No. 35020 was accelerating downhill through the station with the 4.30 p.m. Exeter Central–Waterloo express when the driving axle fractured. *(M.G. Clement Collection)*

'Merchant Navy' Pacific No. 35020 *Bibby Line* on 24 April 1953, showing the damage after the driving axle fractured. The wheel of the fractured axle shows clearly, with the bent coupling rods and the broken brake gear which threw off the brake block. Miraculously no one was killed and the train stayed on the track. Following an investigation into the cause of failure on 12 May 1953, the entire 'Merchant Navy' class was withdrawn from traffic pending ultrasonic inspection of all coupled axles. They were soon cleared and by the end of May only Nos 35020, 35022 and 35028 remained out of service. *(W.S. Rendell)*

During the incident at Crewkerne station when the track was damaged by 'Merchant Navy' class *Bibby Line* No. 35020 breaking an axle, further damage was caused by one of the steel brake blocks, which flew off and hit the iron stanchion on one of the pillars holding up the station canopy. Here you can see the smashed stanchion with the collapsed station canopy. *(M.G. Clement Collection)*

The track damage continued to the east of Crewkerne station, and here the permanent way staff are repairing the damage. *(M.G. Clement Collection)*

The locomotive *Yeovil* was a light Pacific of the 'West Country' class, No. 21C104. The naming ceremony, on 2 November 1945, took place at Yeovil and was attended by members of Southern Railway and local councillors. *Yeovil* was renumbered in May 1948 to 34004, rebuilt in February 1958 and withdrawn from traffic in July 1967. *(M.G. Clement Collection)*

During March 1960 the last steam locomotive built for British Railways left the Swindon works. BR 2–10–0 class '9F' No. 9220 was aptly named *Evening Star*, and is seen here on 20 September 1964 at Yeovil Junction after working a 'Farewell to Steam' rail tour. *(Collectors Corner)*

CHAPTER FIVE

STATIONS & SIGNAL-BOXES

Milborne Port Halt looking west, late 1950s. The signal-box stands in the foreground, with the station buildings behind it. The Down signal on the gantry is in the 'off' position.
(M.G. Clement Collection)

The working of the Somerset and Dorset traffic into Templecombe upper can be seen in this photograph, taken in 1900. The engine was a Somerset and Dorset 0–6–0 goods locomotive built at the Vulcan foundry, and was destined for Bath. The train had come to a halt at No. 2 junction, where the 0–6–0 goods engine had been attached to the rear of the train to draw the coaches and the original train engine back up to Templecombe upper platform. The goods engine would then be uncoupled and the train would wait until departure time for Bath. *(Lens of Sutton)*

The Somerset and Dorset 0–6–0 goods engine has drawn the train up from No. 2 junction and now stands uncoupled at the Templecombe upper platform. The LSWR main line can be seen on the right, with the signal-box for Templecombe in the middle of the platform. The crew chatting and the milk churns on the platform help to make this an above-average pictorial view of Somerset Railways. *(Lens of Sutton)*

Templecombe station, *c.* 1902. For nearly fifty years the railway had monopolised the field of transport and, by the time of this picture, railway traffic was increasing yearly. The motor-car was still the preserve of the wealthy few, and by the end of 1904 the total number of such vehicles had only reached 23,000. Most people travelled by rail, and crowded platforms like this were an everyday occurrence. *(Seaton Museum Photographic Archive)*

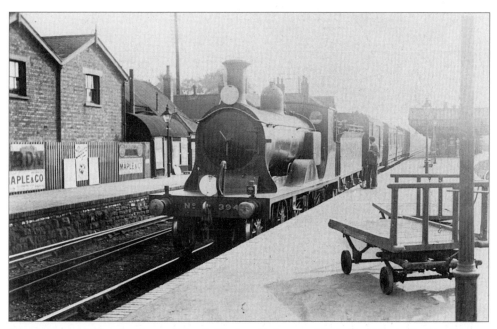

Templecombe station, London and South Western Railway, *c.* 1910. Standing in the Up platform we have a Drummond 'K10' class 4–4–0 mixed traffic engine, No. 394. The 'K10' class numbered forty locomotives which were built between 1900 and 1902. To the right of the train can be seen the Somerset and Dorset joint railway line and Templecombe upper platform. *(Lens of Sutton)*

'King Arthur' class No. 457 *Sir Bedivere*, on a Down West of England stopping train, drifts into Templecombe on a summer day in 1935. The Southern Railway sign warns passengers that they 'must not cross the line here'. *(Seaton Museum Photographic Archive)*

Templecombe, *c.* 1935. At the time of this photograph Templecombe was a busy station, a place where the Somerset and Dorset connected with the Waterloo main line to the west, and a meeting point for trains from all parts of the country. The train in No. 3 platform is waiting to depart for the Somerset and Dorset line. *(Seaton Museum Photographic Archive)*

Templecombe station was rebuilt between 1937 and 1938 by the Southern Railway in the typical style of that time. *(Seaton Museum Photographic Archive)*

Templecombe station, looking east, *c.* 1937. *(M.G. Clement Collection)*

Drummond 'L11' class 4–4–0 No. 30134 light engine with a Southern tender stands beside the water column at the Templecombe lower yard sidings, 9 July 1949. *(H.C. Casserley)*

The Somerset and Dorset joint railway main line ran from Bath Green Park to Bournemouth West via Templecombe and Evercreech Junction. Templecombe is seen here in the 1950s with the Up and Down lines and main platform. On the far left can be seen the Somerset and Dorset lines. *(M.G. Clement Collection)*

Templecombe upper platform, showing the Somerset and Dorset joint railway line curving around on its 33-chain length. The Somerset and Dorset signal-box can be seen on the right, and the Southern line on the extreme right. *(Seaton Museum Photographic Archive)*

Templecombe upper platform, 6 April 1959. British Railways 'Standard' class 4 4–6–0 No. 75011 waits to leave with a train for Bath Green Park station 37 miles 7 chains away. 'Standard' class 4 locomotives were designed by R.A. Riddles and introduced in 1951. *(H.B. Priestley, M.G. Clement Collection)*

We can see by this photograph that in July 1953 Templecombe was thriving. Today the view here has vanished almost without trace. On that summer day nearly fifty years ago a Somerset and Dorset 7F 2–8–0 No. 53809, with a goods train, is standing in the lower yard. Drummond 'H-15' class 4–6–0 mixed traffic engine No. 30334 stands in the siding. *(Geoff Rixon)*

Templecombe lower yard is seen here on 14 August 1958. 'U' class 2–6–0 No. 31794 of Yeovil Shed (72C) approaches from the west on the Up main line, with a stopping train. 'S15' 4–6–0 No. 30847 of Salisbury shed (72B) stands in the yard while Standard class '4' No. 75073 of Weymouth shed (71G) shunts in the lower yard. *(H.B. Priestley, M.G. Clement Collection)*

The Somerset and Dorset main line was from Bath Green Park to Bournemouth West via Evercreech Junction and Templecombe and was affectionately known as the Slow and Dirty. In March 1966 the Somerset and Dorset network was closed. It remained independent to the end and was sadly missed. In this 1960 picture we have Somerset and Dorset class '4F' 0–6–0 No. 44523 standing at platform 3, Templecombe, with a stopping train. *(Roger Joanes, Joanes Publications)*

Templecombe station, looking west, in the early 1960s. The railway network in Somerset was to remain virtually intact until the reshaping of British Railways under the Beeching Report of 1963, which advocated closure of most of the branch lines throughout the country. The result was a disaster for Somerset, and stations like this soon disappeared. *(M.G. Clement Collection)*

Templecombe upper, 11 March 1961. Standard class 5 4–6–0 mixed traffic engine No. 73047 from Bath Green Park shed (82F) with the 9.05 a.m. train to Bath Green Park station. Preparing to work home, the locomotive carries a headlight as a code. *(H.B. Priestley, M.G. Clement Collection)*

To the layman this picture, taken at Templecombe in 1963, is little different from many other railway photographs. For railwaymen it recalls memories of an age now confined to history. GWR 0–6–0 pannier tank No. 4691 was on shunting duty at Templecombe lower yard, and an SR 4–6–0 'S15' class mixed traffic engine No. 30832 has arrived with a Down goods. On the left is the shunter's cabin, and the shunter is in the foreground. On the right, permanent way men are working on the Waterloo main line. *(Gerald Siviour)*

Templecombe engine shed and yard, May 1965. This picture is so rich in information for the railway enthusiast that it compels immediate attention. Standard class 4 No. 80043 keeps company with a Johnson 3F 0–6–0. To the right of the engines 16 ton trucks of locomotive coal stand in the sidings. In the background a large Standard class comes out of the station, assisted by the Standard Pilot engine, with the 3.30 p.m. to Blandford Forum. *(Peter Barnfield)*

Milborne Port signal-box also served as a ticket office when this photograph was taken on 19 August 1962. This box opened on 12 May 1875 and closed on 21 June 1965. *(H.B. Priestley, M.G. Clement Collection)*

Sutton Bingham station looking west from the Down platform. On the Up platform are the main station buildings with the lamp shed at the bottom end. The small shelter and signal-box are on the Down platform. When this picture was taken during the 1950s lighting was still by oil-lamps. *(M.G. Clement Collection)*

The Somerset village of Sutton Bingham lies almost on the border of Dorset, not far from Yeovil. The station was 2 miles 20 chains west of Yeovil Junction and 124 miles 67 chains from Waterloo. Here we see the Down platform, looking west, *c.* 1951. The station was reduced to a halt on 1 August 1960 and the station yard, with sidings, was closed on 31 July 1961. The halt closed on 31 December 1962, but the signal-box remained open until 6 May 1965. *(M.G. Clement Collection)*

Sutton Bingham station, looking Up towards Yeovil Junction, 6 September 1959. There was no footbridge here, so passengers had to cross using the barrow crossing. The platelayers' hut can be seen on the edge of the Down platform. *(M.G. Clement Collection)*

In the days of a shrinking railway system, Sutton Bingham station was closed and today nothing remains. When this picture was taken, Sutton Bingham was still one of those delightful Southern Region stations in rural Somerset. *(M.G. Clement Collection)*

The evocative quality of Somerset railways is shown in this picture of Yeovil Pen Mill, 13 August 1958. The name-board reads 'Yeovil Pen Mill change for Taunton and Exeter'. In the platform is a Western Region Railbus with 'N' class No. 31791 *The Station Pilot*. *(H.B. Priestley, M.G. Clement Collection)*

Yeovil Town engine shed from Ninesprings Hill, 12 June 1938. In the foreground are Drummond 4–4–0 'K10' class No. 389; Maunsell 'N' class 2–6–0 No. 1829; and Drummond 'L11' class No. 163. The other locomotives look like Drummond engines. *(National Railway Museum)*

Royal Blue Bournemouth service coach No. 2222 is pictured outside British Railways Yeovil Town station on 17 August 1964. The summer of 1964 was the last time that a complete service worked by steam ran on the Salisbury–Exeter line. *(Pamlin Prints)*

A fine picture of 'West Country' class Pacific No. 34030 *Watersmeet* at Yeovil Town shed during the early 1960s. Ninesprings Hill is in the background. *(M.G. Clement Collection)*

A busy scene at Yeovil Town station, 17 August 1964. At the left is the Yeovil Town signal-box, with the station buildings and platforms standing behind. Beyond that the line goes up to serve Yeovil Junction and on the far right are pictured the sidings buildings, with the locomotive shed of Yeovil MPD. *(Pamlin Prints)*

A photograph of Yeovil Town station taken eighty years before the photograph above. Yeovil Town station, on the main line from Waterloo, was then run by the London and South Western, which continued until 1923, when the London and South Western and the Midland were grouped into the Southern and the LMS. Many changes can be seen between the two pictures. The scene around the station area and the buildings is much altered, but the locomotive sheds look much the same. *(Seaton Museum Photographic Archive)*

Crewkerne station during the London and South Western Railway era. The picture, looking westward, is from a postcard postmarked 1906 and shows at least eleven staff members lined up on the platform. *(M.G. Clement Collection)*

The distinctive quality of Crewkerne station in the days of the Southern Railway is captured in this photograph, which clearly shows the station layout. The footbridge is in the foreground, with the Up platform, the goods shed, the LSWR signal-box and the Up and Down sidings. The Southern Railway poster advertises Ramsgate and the other poster informs passengers that Vim 'cleans and polishes'. *(Seaton Museum Photographic Archive)*

Crewkerne Gates, one of the many crossings of this type in Somerset, was soon to become a part of railway history, when replaced with electronic barriers. The crossing-gates, seen here in 1964, have a big red oil-lamp for night and a big red disc with white surround for daytime. On the far left of the picture can be seen the crossing-keeper's cabin. *(M.G. Clement Collection)*

Another 1964 view of Crewkerne Gates, viewed from the Up track side. The Crewkerne Gates sign is on the Down side of the double track main line, and next to it is the lengthman's hut. *(M.G. Clement Collection)*

The Westinghouse Brake and Signal Company frame at Crewkerne Gates in 1964. Working from left to right, they operated: 1. Up distant; 2. Up home; 3. Down home; on 4 and 5 the plates are missing, but we presume that 4 would be the locking lever and 5 the Down distant.
(M.G. Clement Collection)

This dilapidated box housed an important piece of railway equipment: the communication telephone. In 1964 this one could be found beside the Crewkerne Gates. It was a type that was at that time used in stations and signal-boxes throughout the Southern Railway. The earpiece hung on a cord to the left, with the mouthpiece in the centre. A small plunger was used to ring a series of bell codes. Each location had its own bell code, and the list of these can be seen on the left of the box.
(M.G. Clement Collection)

Railway photographers certainly believe in taking unusual pictures. This one, of a semaphore signal arm in the 'off' position, was taken from the top of the Down signal post at Crewkerne Gates in 1964.
(M.G. Clement Collection)

The late winter sunshine casts long shadows over Crewkerne station in this nostalgic view taken in 1964.
(M.G. Clement Collection)

Crewkerne, with its lovely old stone houses and streets that lead down to the Market Square, is a busy town on the main road to Yeovil. The station, photographed here in 1983 by Mike Clement, is on the Salisbury to Exeter line and, apart from the new station signs, has changed very little since it was built in the 1860s. *(M.G. Clement Collection)*

Crewkerne station from the footbridge, August 1983. It presents a sorry sight. The single track on the Up side still stretches away to Yeovil, but the Down platform stands disused, with weeds growing up through the platform. The track has gone on the Down side, the signal-box stands empty and all the sidings have gone. *(M.G. Clement Collection)*

This old London South Western signal-box at Chard Junction, August 1983, was taken out of service, with the old gates, on 7 January 1968. A brand new box, with a passing loop, was installed and new full barriers came into use on 14 January 1968. *(M.G. Clement Collection)*

This view of Hewish Gates in 1964 was taken with the crossing-gates open to road traffic. Hewish Gates was 134 miles 4 chains from Waterloo. *(M.G. Clement Collection)*

Hewish Gates, 1964. The signal-box is on the Up side, with the Up signal guarding the gates, which are open to road traffic. The crossing-keeper's cottage is on the other side of the gates. On the Down side are the Down semaphore signals and in the foreground are stop blocks on the Down siding. All that remains of this location today are the two half-barriers and a single track. *(M.G. Clement Collection)*

Chard Junction *c.* 1952. 'King Arthur' class 4–6–0 No. 30449 *Sir Torre* sweeps into the station with a Down Templecombe–Exeter Central train. The locomotive is just passing over the level-crossing and on the left you can see the signal-box. Behind the box is the Chard Road Tavern. When the station first opened it was known as Chard Road. *(H.B. Priestley, M.G. Clement Collection)*

Chard Junction, *c.* 1952. This picture, taken from the branch platform, shows the main station buildings on the right. In the background the main line curves away to the right, and next to the branch line stop blocks is a platelayers' hut. Prominent in the background stands the Chard Road Tavern. *(M.G. Clement Collection)*

Chard Junction Down platform, showing station buildings, *c.* 1955. Behind the station can be seen the Down sidings and minerals wagons. The chimney-stack and buildings behind are Wilts United Dairies. Wilts United Dairies attracted national attention on 11 June 1958 when it produced a then world record 104 tons of butter in one day. *(M.G. Clement Collection)*

As memories of the lines that closed fade into history, photographs like this become more important. This is one of Mike Clement's favourite photographs: Chard Junction in 18 May 1959. 'West Country' class No. 34034 *Honiton*, sitting in the station, is working an Up stopping train. The two heavy four-wheeled barrows, the sack trucks, the posters, the parcel office, the level-crossing warning sign and the signal-box are all long gone. *(R.J. Sellick)*

On a cold, wet, winter day in 1961, 0–6–0 pannier tank No. 4622 runs into Chard Junction branch terminus. In the background the line curves around, back to Chard Central station. *(C.L. Caddy)*

Chard Junction is pictured here on 9 January 1962. The camera has captured 'West Country' class Pacific No. 34092 *City of Wells* working the Down 12.35 p.m. Salisbury–Exeter Central stopping train. *(H.C Casserley)*

The station nameboard reads 'Chard Junction, change for Chard'. In this excellent picture, taken during July 1962, 'Merchant Navy' class No. 35030 *Elder Dempster Lines* thunders through on a thirteen-coach Exeter Central–Waterloo express. To the left and below the station nameboard you can just see the box on the lamp-post for the shunting bell to the signal-box. *(Peter Barnfield)*

A look inside the new signal-box at Chard Junction, showing the new computerised panel and track with passing loop, August 1983. *(M.G. Clement Collection)*

Chard Junction, looking west towards Axminster, 1987. Nothing remains of the Up and Down station buildings, or the Down platform. To the right of the old Up platform you can just get a glimpse of the old goods shed. *(M.G. Clement Collection)*

A far cry from the days of steam: Chard Junction looking west after closure. The Up side station buildings and goods shed still remain intact, but the station canopy has gone, along with the overhead foot bridge. The Down side platform and buildings have completely gone. *(M.G. Clement Collection)*

This excellent railway picture, full of much detailed information, shows the layout of Chard Town (LSWR), 1 June 1953. The goods shed is on the left, with the line going into it. On the right are the sidings with the goods office on the far right in the distance. In the station yard there are two double-decker buses. *(R.J. Sellick)*

Chard Town goods office and yard, with the goods shed on the right. The mineral wagon standing in the yard had a carrying capacity of 16 tons. Bags of coal stand on the right-hand side of the yard. The line continues out to join the Chard branch. *(M.G. Clement Collection)*

Chard Central station, 1952. The LSWR reached Chard Central by a loop line, and the line closed to passenger traffic on 10 September 1962. Shown here is Churchward 2–6–0 tank of the '45XX' class, No. 5503, with the 1.35 p.m. to Taunton, awaiting the right of way. *(H.B. Priestley, M.G. Clement Collection)*

The pre-war signal-box at Chard Central, 3 September 1958. *(A.E. West, M.G. Clement Collection)*

Chard Central, seen here on 12 September 1959, was once known as Chard Joint station because before the name change on 1 February 1928 it was part of both the London and South Western Railway and the Great Western. *(M.G. Clement Collection)*

Chard Central station, 8 April 1962, in the days of the Southern Region of British Railways. *(C.L. Caddy)*

The 0–6–0 pannier tank No. 8783 is pictured at Ilminster station on 8 September 1962 with its two-coach train, *en route* for Taunton. On the left is the tall signal-box, with wagons in the sidings beside it. *(C.L. Caddy)*

A general view of a station with the delightful name of Thornfalcon, spring 1962. The station was on the Chard–Taunton branch line, and this view was taken from the road bridge. The station is on the left of the branch line, and there is a small crane standing in the sidings. *(C.L. Caddy)*

The first steam railway to reach Somerset was the Bristol and Exeter Railway, which reached Taunton on 1 July 1842. By the end of the nineteenth century the Great Western Railway dominated the West of England and was known for its complete dependability. Its passing to British Railways on 31 December 1947 was a sad day for its many admirers. Taunton station, with the main line on the right, is seen here in 1961. A pannier tank of the '57XX' series, No. 4622, is standing in the Chard branch platform. *(C.L. Caddy)*

Taunton station, on the GWR main line, was 18 miles 44 chains from Chard Junction, on the Southern. British Railways standard class 3 2–6–2 tank No. 82008 is seen here on 14 April 1962 in charge of the Chard branch train. *(C.L. Caddy)*

CHAPTER SIX

BRANCH LINES

*Standard class 3 2–6–2 tank No. 82030, 14 April 1962. She heads out of Chard Central for
Chard Junction, with cylinder cocks blowing, with a parcel van and two coaches. (C.L. Caddy)*

Chard Junction looking west towards Axminster. This photograph, taken during the summer of 1913, is charged with interest. The photographer successfully captured the atmosphere of those pre-First World War days, with passengers waiting for the train. The large enamel-on-metal advertising boards on display were designed to make an immediate impact, and are highly collectable today. *(Seaton Museum Photographic Archive)*

Chard Junction again, in 1935, then under the Southern Railway. This picture was taken looking Up towards Crewkerne. In the sidings beside the goods shed are box wagons, parcel vans and newspaper vans. *(Seaton Museum Photographic Archive)*

In this picture, taken on 2 March 1956, we are given the information on the station sign that this is Chard Junction, where you can change for Chard. The branch was operated by the Southern and Western regions and connected at Taunton station. Before the closure of the branch lines, cross-country routes were a part of the Somerset rural scene. *(R.M. Casserley)*

Chard Junction station, 2 August 1951. To the right on the branch line is the goods shed with canopy and on the left the branch signal-box. *(R.J. Sellick)*

The railway network in Somerset was to remain virtually intact until the reshaping of British Railways under the Beeching Report of 1963, which advocated closure of most of the branch lines throughout the country. This is Chard Central station in 1959, not long before the station closure which took place in 1962. Judging by the appearance of the station at this time, inevitable decline had already taken place. *(M.G. Clement Collection)*

Chard Town station, on the London and South Western Railway, only had a short, single passenger platform, with a small station building of corrugated iron. The first train in the town arrived at Chard Town station on 8 May 1863. The LSWR reached Chard Central by a loop line and the loop-line platform is pictured here in June 1953. The LSWR station at Chard Town closed on 1 January 1917, but the goods yard remained open until the branch line closed on 3 October 1966. *(R.J. Sellick)*

The old Chard Central station building is still standing but in August 1987, when this picture was taken, it was part of a tyre depot. *(M.G. Clement Collection)*

A first-rate photograph of Chard Junction, showing the branch layout, 1952. On the right stands the branch signal-box and the run-around loop can be seen to come back on the branch train. The line to the Up sidings can be seen going behind the signal-box. *(M.G. Clement Collection)*

Chard Junction station, 1961. Working the branch train is 0–6–0 pannier tank No. 4622 of the 57XX class. The train, with its two coaches, is waiting to depart bunker first for Chard Central. *(C.L. Caddy)*

Western 0–6–0 pannier tank No. 4663 with its two-coach train, *en route* for Chard Central, runs into the platform at Donyatt Halt bunker first, 8 September 1962. Donyatt Halt was opened on 5 May 1928 and had a single platform edged with sleepers and a small wooden shelter. It closed on the day this photograph was taken. *(C.L. Caddy)*

Hurrying away from Hatch with its two-coach train, pannier tank No. 4663 of the '57XX' class is *en route* for Taunton, *c.* 1960. The railway was then an essential part of the Somerset country life and pictures like this are full of nostalgia for days long gone. Hatch was on the Chard branch line and locomotives working the branch line were from the WR shed at Taunton (83B). *(C.L. Caddy)*

Ilton Halt was on the GWR Chard Central to Taunton branch line, a distance of 1 mile 27 chains up the line from Ilminster. This small halt served a rural community and was opened on 26 May 1920. It fell foul of Dr Beeching in 1962. *(C.L. Caddy)*

Pannier tank No. 4663, in charge of a two-coach train, runs into Hatch station, 8 September 1962. Hatch station was on the Chard to Taunton line, 3 miles 26 chains east of Ilton Halt. *(C.L. Caddy)*

Departing Donyatt Halt for Chard Central, pannier tank No. 4663 is working bunker first with its two-coach train, 8 September 1962. The guard's van is next to the engine. *(C.L. Caddy)*

C.B. Collett's '57XX' class locomotives were introduced to the Great Western Railway in 1929 to become the standard shunting and general purpose tank engines. Here, during the summer of 1962, No. 8783 of that class runs into Thornfalcon station, bunker first. *(C.L. Caddy)*

Another of the Somerset stations that were closed under the Beeching axe. Stations like Ilminster, pictured here during September 1962, gave rural communities a contact with the outside world. Today, with ever increasing road traffic, people realise that the Beeching axe cut too deep. Ilminster station was 58 chains up the line from Donyatt Halt, and waiting at the station is 0–6–0 pannier tank No. 8783, with its two-coach train. *(C.L. Caddy)*

Pannier tank '57XX' class No. 9647 approaches Ilminster from Donyatt Halt with an Up goods train, 14 April 1962. The shed plate on the smoke-box door reads 83B, confirming that the engine is from the Taunton shed. Ilminster station was opened on 11 September 1866 and closed on 8 September 1962. *(C.L. Caddy)*

Yeovil Town station, 1958. The signal-box is on the right, with Southern Maunsell 'S15' class 4–6–0 No. 30826 waiting in the siding. The 2–6–2 Western Tank of Churchward 45XX class No. 5543 is preparing to leave for Taunton via Yeovil Pen Mill. Sadly, all that can be seen here now is a large car park. *(H.B. Priestley, M.G. Clement Collection)*

The Dugald Drummond 4–4–0 mixed traffic engines of the 'K10' class were classic, elegant locomotives. At Yeovil Town on 15 September 1948 is veteran No. 152 in Southern livery, towards the end of its working life. No. 152 came into service in December 1902 and was withdrawn from traffic in February 1949. At the Yeovil shed in 1939 they still had five engines of this class left, Nos 143/5/52 and 340/44. They worked three booked duties, shunting the Town and Junction yards, shunting at Chard and Templecombe and goods to Pen Mill and Templecombe. *(A.E. West, M.G. Clement Collection)*

A perfect country railway scene in which Adams '0–2' class 0–4–4 tank No. E196, fitted for pull-and-push working, from Yeovil Junction drifts into Yeovil Town with the branch train, 2 August 1928. *(H.C. Casserley)*

Standing outside Yeovil Town shed, with the water tank in the background, we have British Railways 'Standard' class 4 4–6–0 mixed traffic engine of the '75000' class, No. 75020. Mike Clement, ex-cleaner and fireman, comments that this engine looks in need of a good clean. *(Collectors Corner)*

Rural Somerset and the meandering train combine to make this an outstanding picture of days now long gone. 'M-7' 0–4–4 Drummond tank No. 30129, fitted for pull-and-push working, heads its two-coach branch train from Yeovil Junction into Yeovil Town, 12 July 1902. *(C.J. Gammell)*

The beauty of the Somerset countryside is captured in this photograph, taken from Penn Hill on 12 July 1962 by C.J. Gammell. It is a picture that conjures up those far-gone days when steam locomotives slipped gently along country branch lines, and the railway was an essential part of country life. A Drummond 0–4–4 'M7' tank No. 30129, with its two-coach pull-and-push train, is meandering out of Yeovil Town towards Yeovil Junction with its tail-lamp on the bottom left of the buffer beam. The GWR main line to Weymouth can be seen running through the cutting on the far left. *(C.J. Gammell)*

This view was taken in 1964 from Crewkerne Gates Down signal post, looking back Up the main line eastwards towards Crewkerne, a distance of 51 chains, from gates to station. *(M.G. Clement Collection)*

BURNHAM-ON-SEA
(Somerset)
Map Sq. 22.
Pop. 5,120. Clos. day Wed.
From Paddington via Bristol and High-
bridge 146¼ miles.
1st cl.—Single 49/9, Mth. Ret. 59/11.
3rd cl.—Single 29/10, Mth. Ret. 39/11.

Padd.	Burn.	Burn.	Padd.
a.m.		a.m.	
5 30	11 20	6 50r	11 20
7 30sr	12 57	9 40r	2 20
9 15r	1 55	11 30sr	4 25
11 15r	3 50	11 30r	5 45
p.m.		p.m.	
1 15r	5 50	2 35er	6 40
1 18	6 35	2 35r	8 15
2 15	7 15	4 0	9 35
11 50e	9 35	6 45	4 15
—	—	7 25	7 25
—	—	—	—

Sunday Trains.

p.m.			
11 50	9 35	—	—

e Not Sat.   s Sat. only.
r Refresh. Car.

Another Route
From Waterloo via Templecombe 146¾
miles. Same fares.

W'loo	Burn.	Burn.	W'loo
a.m.		a.m.	
1 25	9 35	6 50r	11 46
9 0r	2 25	9 40r	2 29
p.m.		p.m.	
12 50r	5 50	2 5r	6 40
2 50r	7 15	4 0r	8 38
—	—	6 45†	3 55
—	—	—	—

No Sunday Trains.
† Via Eastleigh.   r Refresh. Car.
e Not Sat.   s Sat. only.
Bus facilities. From Highbridge, Railway Stn., approx. half-hourly
Weekday, hourly Sun. p.m., 8 min.
journey.

A 1949 timetable for Burnham-on-Sea.

CHAPTER SEVEN

THE END OF THE LINE

Some twenty-one years after the closure of the Slow and Dirty, you can still see a well-defined trackbed in this 1987 photograph. It follows the hedge on the right to run underneath the London and South Western railway main line, seen in the distance. Templecombe village and church can be seen on the far left. (M.G. Clement Collection)

Templecombe shed, April 1961. In the foreground are five Johnson '3F' 0–6–0 freight engines standing in storage. They were introduced in 1903 by the Midland Railway, and the nearest engine to the camera is No. 43682. In the background is Standard class 5 4–6–0 No. 73047 and Stanier 2–6–2 class 3MT tank engine No. 40126. *(G.A. Richardson)*

Looking work-weary and begrimed, these four Johnson 0–6–0 freight engines, their fires long gone out, their boilers stone cold, look a sorry sight as they wait in storage at Templecombe shed, April 1961. Introduced to the Somerset and Dorset in 1896, engine No. 43216 in the foreground was one of Johnson's original 1875 design. In the background, on the Southern main line, 'Merchant Navy' class No. 35028 *Clan Line* thunders by on a Waterloo–West of England express. *(G.A. Richardson)*

During its days of glory, Templecombe station was a passing place for trains such as the Atlantic Coast Express, and here holiday traffic bound for the West Country would leave the Somerset and Dorset to run on to Exeter and beyond. Year after year the pageant swept in some fresh form along the metalled track, until that sad day in March 1966 when the Somerset and Dorset closed. These 1983 photographs show that nothing remains of the station buildings and only the signal-box is left standing. Long gone are the large Up and Down marshalling yards, the engine shed and the Somerset and Dorset Railway. *(M.G. Clement Collection)*

This overgrown railway bridge near Templecombe passed over the old Somerset and Dorset line, but nature now appears to have taken over, and trees grow where trains once passed. *(M.G. Clement Collection)*

Sutton Bingham station Down side, 24 August 1983. The station is only a hollow shell of its former self; all that is left are the crumbling remains of the old platelayers' hut and the tool shed. *(M.G. Clement Collection)*

The importance of railways to rural communities in Victorian Somerset lay in the contact they provided with the outside world. The development of the steam locomotive led to a network of railway lines spreading across the county, which played an important role in transport. Unfortunately, the relative economies of road and rail transport resulted in the Beeching reorganisation and by the 1960s over one-third of the network had disappeared. This picture was taken on 24 August 1983 and it seems impossible to believe that the asphalt of this council car park was once part of the layout of Yeovil Town station and yard. An order has dissolved here and the hand of time has rested cruelly on this scene to relegate over a hundred years of steam to history. We now look back at the age of steam with nostalgia, but time has shown that mistakes were made, and if this network still existed much pressure would be taken from the deserts of asphalt that make up our motorways and bypasses. *(M.G. Clement Collection)*

A view of the short-lived Crewkerne new signal-box. This box opened under the Southern Region on 6 November 1960, and was closed on 26 February 1967 following a Western Region takeover, which resulted in a downgrading of the Salisbury–Exeter line. *(M.G. Clement Collection)*

Crewkerne crossing on 24 July 1983. The crossing-keeper's house is now a private residence. *(M.G. Clement Collection)*

The stanchion informs us that this is Crewkerne crossing, 132.3 miles from Waterloo. Here in 1983 only memories remain of a whole lost order of things. *(M.G. Clement Collection)*

Long grass and unkempt bushes grow on what were once railwaymen's tidy gardens. This picture was taken on Sunday 10 July 1983 and shows the electronic barriers that replaced the gates at Hewish. Long gone are the gates, the signal-box, the double track main line and the signalman, who was always ready with a friendly wave at passing trains. *(M.G. Clement Collection)*

Old permanent way men would turn in their graves at the present condition of the single track side at Hewish Gates. *(M.G. Clement Collection)*

Chard Central station, looking Up towards Donyatt, 1950s. The water tank is visible through the large station canopy, with the Chard Central signal-box in the background. *(H.B. Priestley, M.G. Clement Collection)*

Chard Central station, 30 September 1958. The water tank is in the centre, starter signals are at the left, and the engine shed is in the background. *(A.E. West, M.G. Clement Collection)*

Chard Central station, 1 September 1962. Pannier tank No. 3736 prepares to depart, with its three-coach train, for Chard Junction. With the Beeching cut only a few days away it can be seen that the run-down of a small station doomed to closure had already begun. *(C.L. Caddy)*

Chard Junction, 1983. Electronic barriers have replaced the old crossing-gates and a new signal-box has replaced the old LSWR box. *(M.G. Clement Collection)*

This view of Chard Central station was taken during the summer of 1987. The station closed on 16 September 1962 and, despite major changes, the railway station is still recognisable. *(M.G. Clement Collection)*

One of the most immediate visual results of the closure of the railways was the rapid decline of the stations, as seen here in the summer of 1987 at Chard Junction. The old goods shed on the Down side now appears to be a storage depot for a furniture removal firm, and the track side is covered with weeds. *(M.G. Clement Collection)*

In 1923 over one hundred railway companies grouped together to form the 'big four': the Great Western Railway, the London Midland and Scottish, the Southern Railway and the London and North Eastern. Other lines, such as the Somerset and Dorset Joint Railway, continued independently. The trespass warning sign belonging to that company is now a highly collectable item. *(Peter Barnfield)*

ACKNOWLEDGEMENTS

We are grateful to all those who have helped in the compilation of this book by contributing valuable information.

Mike would like to thank many of his old railway colleagues who have given him so much of their time in recalling details of days now long gone, and for the loan of photographs. Special thanks to Tom and Nellie Salter, Gerald and Janet Russell, Sid and Margaret Dunn, David Pettitt, John Gilham, Stephen Townroe, Hubert Pike and Singleton Gillham.

We are indebted to the photographers, both amateur and professional, whose pictures illustrate this book, visually capturing the age of steam. They include: Peter Barnfield, C.J. Gammell, H.C. and R.M. Casserley, H.B. Priestley, C.L. Caddy, the National Railway Museum, R. Dyer, G.W. Sharpe, Lens of Sutton, Roger Joanes, G.A. Richardson, W.S. Rendell and many others.

We are grateful to our wives, Doris and Carol, for their encouragement, and to Lyn Marshall for her assistance with the compilation of the book. We would like to thank Simon Fletcher of Sutton Publishing for his assistance.

The pictures in this book come from the superb collection of railway photographs belonging to Mike Clement, He would like to thank leading porter Ralph Watkins, Lyme Regis, who took a staff photograph in 1961 which included Mike; this was the inspiration for Mike's railway collection.

Ted Gosling
Mike Clement